MW00334410

S.I.P.
SHELTER IN PLACE

A Cocktail Guide and Reference
for Making Craft Cocktails at Home

C. Emma Creese

Louis J McNerney and Brad Smith

Copyright © 2021 Louis J McNerney and Brad Smith
All rights reserved
First Edition

Fulton Books, Inc.
Meadville, PA

Published by Fulton Books 2021

ISBN 978-1-64952-830-8 (paperback)
ISBN 978-1-63985-143-0 (hardcover)
ISBN 978-1-64952-831-5 (digital)

Printed in the United States of America

This book is a companion publication of *In Lou of Going Out*, a cookbook inspired by the pandemic. We have all been asked to stay home and "shelter in place" to the best of our abilities during this crisis.

I was inspired to put together cocktail guide for folks to enjoy popular drinks in the comfort of their own home. All you need are basic bar supplies to create many of the cocktails you enjoy when you are out on the town.

I hope you enjoy this collection, and it helps make the current situation more bearable and perhaps even enjoyable as you venture into the world of concocting craft cocktails.

Basic Bar Supplies

Jigger
: a two-sided measuring cup (1 oz side and 2 oz side) to help pour the right amount of the alcohol or mixer for the perfect pour

Shaker
: A shaker is used to quickly mix a drink's ingredients; its metal composition drives down the temperature and dilutes the ice to give it balance. When a drink is not stirred or blended, you have to shake it to wake it.

Muddler
: Think of the muddler as the pestle of the bar world. Used to extract juice from fruit pulp and essential oils from herbs and citrus peels, there is not a substitute out there that is as efficient. Not all muddlers are created equally, and variations exist in material, shape, and texture. Basically, it all boils down to wood versus a dishwasher-safe material like plastic or metal, tooth grip or smooth, and width/length. For most home use a plastic dishwasher safe version works best.

Bar spoon
: A proper bar spoon is tall enough for a cocktail glass, often with a twisted handle that makes circular moves smooth and steady. It may be adorned with a decorative end with which to move the ingredients. The spoon end can be used to measure out the appropriate amount of bitters, syrups, or liqueurs needed in your drink.

Mixing glass
: A mixing glass lets your guests see the booze swirling and magic happening. A pint glass works well however there are fancier versions available with a pouring spout design.

Strainer
: The chief job of the cocktail strainer is separating liquid from solid—that sounds easy enough, but choosing the wrong one can leave you with a mouth full of annoying mint bits. There are two types: Julep and Hawthorne. The *Hawthorne* strainer has a flat, perforated face framed by a coil that sifts out ice and other particulates. The coil's convenient secondary function works as a flexible spring, allowing the strainer to fit over glassware of various sizes. The *julep* strainer is a curved disc of perforated steel that looks kind of like a flattened thimble with a handle. The rule of thumb is to use the julep strainer for stirred drinks and the Hawthorne for shaken drinks.

Garnishing Tools

Peeler	A small handheld kitchen peeler should be sharp enough to render precise thin cuts from only the aromatic peel layer rather than the bitter white pith. Choose one with a pivoting edge.
Zester	Several drinks call for zest to add a finishing flavor.
Microplane grater	used for finishing touches like nutmeg, cinnamon, cardamom to complete the cocktail

A basic well for mixing drinks.

Most bars have what the call a well. Well liquor is the lower cost alcohols that are used to make 90 percent of the cocktails produced on any given night. Unless a specific brand of vodka, gin, whiskey, etc. is requested, the well brand will be used. A well consists of the following elements:

Sweet Vermouth	Dry Vermouth
Brandy	Rum
Scotch	Gin
Vodka	Whiskey
Tequila	Triple Sec
Simple Syrup	Agave
Sweet and Sour Mix	Grenadine
Ginger Beer	Cranberry Juice
Orange Juice	Grapefruit Juice
Olive Brine	Lemon Juice
Lime Juice	Cherry Juice
Lemon Wedges and Twists	Lime Wedges
Olives	Cherries
Pearl Onions	

This may seem like a lot to have in stock, but it really isn't if you want to provide a full range of cocktails for your guests. In this book, you will be able to make a variety of cocktails using these ingredients that will impress even your most precocious attendee.

Vodka Cocktails

Vodka cocktails use the neutral taste of vodka to blend seamlessly with just about anything.

Vodka and Tonic
> 1 1/2 oz vodka
> Tonic
> Wedge lime
>
> Fill highball glass with ice
> Add vodka, top with tonic
> Garnish with lime wedge

Dirty Vodka Martini
> 2 1/2 oz vodka
> 1/2 oz dry vermouth
> 1/2 oz olive brine
> 2 to 4 olives
>
> Add all the ingredients into a mixing glass with ice and stir.
> Strain into a chilled cocktail glass.
> Garnish with two to four olives, skewered.

Moscow Mule
> 2 oz vodka
> 1 oz fresh lime juice
> Ginger beer, to top
> Lime wedge
>
> Usually made in a copper mug (or stainless steel).
> Fill a chilled-mug with ice.
> Add vodka, lime juice with ice and stir.
> Top with ginger beer.
> Garnish with a lime wedge.

Kamakazi
>   2 oz vodka
>   3/4 oz orange liqueur
>   3/4 oz fresh lime juice

Makes two shots.
Add all the ingredients into a shaker with ice and shake thoroughly until well-chilled.
Strain into two shot glasses.

Blue Hawaii
>   3/4 oz vodka
>   3/4 oz light rum
>   1/2 oz blue curacao
>   3 oz pineapple juice
>   1 oz sweet and sour mix
>   Pineapple wedge
>   Umbrella

Add all ingredients into a shaker with ice and shake until well chilled (or blend all ingredients with ice in a blender).
Strain into a tall glass over crushed or pebble ice (or pour from blender into glass with no ice).
Garnish with a pineapple wedge and cocktail umbrella.

Bloody Mary
>   2 oz vodka
>   4 oz tomato juice
>   1/2 oz freshly squeezed lemon juice
>   6 dashes tabasco
>   2 pinches freshly ground black pepper
>   4 dashes Worcestershire sauce
>   Salt
>   Celery stalk
>   Lime wedge

Pour the salt onto a small plate.
Rub the juicy side of a lime wedge along the lip of a pint glass, rim the glass with the salt, and fill the glass with ice.
Add the remaining ingredients into a shaker with ice and shake until chilled.
Strain into the prepared glass, and garnish with a celery stalk and lime wedge.

Vodka and Cranberry (a.k.a. Cape Codder)
>   1 1/2 oz vodka
>   Cranberry juice, to top
>   Lime wedge
>   Add the vodka into a highball glass over ice.
>   Top with cranberry juice and stir until chilled.
>   Squeeze a lime wedge over the glass and drop it into the drink.

Apple Cranberry Martini
>   2 oz vodka
>   1 oz cran-apple juice
>   1/4 oz fresh lime juice
>   Ginger beer, to top
>   Cranberries
>   Apple slices
>
>   Pour the first three ingredients into a mule mug and add ice.
>   Top with ginger beer.
>   Garnish with fresh cranberries and apple slices.

Black Russian
>   2 oz vodka
>   1 oz Kahlúa
>
>   Add all the ingredients into a mixing glass with ice and stir.
>   Strain into an old-fashioned glass over fresh ice.

Cucumber Gimlet
>   1/2 oz vodka
>   2 slices cucumber (1/4-inch slices)
>   1 1/2 fresh basil leaves
>   1 oz lemonade
>   1/4 oz lime juice, freshly squeezed
>   Basil leaf
>
>   Muddle the basil and cucumber in a shaker.
>   Add remaining ingredients and ice and shake.
>   Strain into a rocks glass over ice.
>   Garnish with a basil leaf.

Cosmopolitan

    1 1/2 oz citrus vodka

    1 oz Cointreau

    1/2 oz fresh lime juice

    1 dash cranberry juice

    Lime wheel

    Add all ingredients into a shaker with ice and shake.

    Strain into a chilled cocktail glass.

    Garnish with a lime wheel.

Expresso Martini

    2 oz vodka

    1/2 oz simple syrup

    1/2 oz coffee liqueur

    1 oz freshly brewed espresso

    Coffee beans

    Add all the ingredients into a shaker with ice and shake.

    Fine strain into a chilled martini glass.

    Garnish with three coffee beans

Screwdriver

    1 1/2 oz vodka

    3 oz orange juice

    Fill highball glass with ice.

    Add vodka and orange juice.

    Stir and serve.

Gin Cocktails

Dirty Gin Martini
> 2 1/2 oz gin
> 1/2 oz dry vermouth
> 1/2 oz olive brine
> 2 to 4 olives

> Add all the ingredients into a mixing glass with ice and stir.
> Strain into a chilled cocktail glass.
> Garnish with two to four olives, skewered.

Negroni
> 1 oz gin
> 1 oz Campari
> 1 oz sweet vermouth
> Orange peel

> Add all the ingredients into a mixing glass with ice and stir until well chilled.
> Strain into a rocks glass filled with large ice cubes.
> Garnish with an orange peel.

Bee's Knees
> 2 oz gin
> 3/4 oz fresh lemon juice
> Honey syrup
> Lemon twist

> Add all ingredients into a shaker with ice and shake.
> Strain into a chilled martini glass.
> Garnish with a lemon twist.

Gin Sonic
>1 1/2 oz Gin
>2 1/4 oz club soda
>2 1/4 oz tonic water
>Lemon twist

>Combine all ingredients in a highball glass over ice.
>Garnish with a lemon twist.

Greyhound
>1 1/2 oz dry gin
>4 oz grapefruit juice

>In a highball glass over ice, combine gin and grapefruit juice
>Stir well.

Salty Dog
>Same as above just add a salted rim to the glass

Gin Gimlet
>2 oz gin
>2 oz lime juice
>1/4 oz simple syrup

>Place sugar in a shallow dish; dip rim of chilled glass into sugar so rim is coated.
>Scoop ice into a shaker. Pour gin and lime juice over the ice and shake well. Pour drink into prepared glass.

Tom Collins
>2 oz gin
>2 oz lemon juice
>1 oz simple syrup
>1 dash Angostura bitters
>Club soda
>Lemon slice
>Cherry

>Fill a cocktail shaker with ice.
>Pour in the gin, lemon juice, simple syrup, and a dash of bitters.
>Cover and shake until the outside of the container is frosty, about 15 seconds.
>Strain into a highball glass full of ice.
>Top off with club soda and garnish with a lemon slice and maraschino cherry.

French 75
>   2 oz gin
>   1 teaspoon simple syrup
>   1/2 oz lemon juice
>   5 oz brut champagne
>   Lemon slice

>   Chill cocktail shaker and glass (champagne flute) in the freezer.
>   Add ice to shaker.
>   Pour gin, simple syrup, and lemon juice into shaker. Shake well.
>   Fill chilled glass half full of ice, then strain cocktail into the glass.
>   Top with champagne and garnish with a lemon slice.

Ramos Gin Fizz
>   2 oz gin
>   1/2 oz sweet and sour mix
>   2 oz half-and-half
>   1 oz simple syrup
>   1 oz triple sec
>   1 oz orange juice
>   Club soda

>   Fill a cocktail shaker with ice.
>   Pour in gin, half-and-half, sweet-and-sour mix, orange juice, triple sec.
>   Shake vigorously; rest a second, then shake a little more.
>   Strain into a tall cocktail glass.
>   Top off with club soda.

Rum Cocktails

Daiquiri
> 2 oz light rum
> 1 oz fresh lime juice
> 3/4 oz simple syrup
> Lime twist

> Add all the ingredients into a shaker with ice, and shake until well-chilled.
> Strain into a chilled coupe.
> Garnish with a lime twist.

Dark Storm
> 2 oz dark rum
> 1/2 oz lime juice, freshly squeezed
> Ginger beer, to top (about 5 ounces)
> Lime wedge

> Fill a tall glass with ice.
> Add rum and lime juice
> Top with the ginger beer.
> Garnish with a lime wedge.

Cuba Libre
> 1 oz rum
> 3 oz Coca-Cola
> Lime wedge

> Add all the ingredients to a highball glass filled with ice.
> Garnish with a lime wedge.

Nightcap
>   2oz rum
>   2 oz cold brewed coffee
>   1/2 oz maple syrup
>   Orange zest
>   1 dash Angostura bitters
>   Tonic water
>   Orange peel

Add all ingredients except the tonic into a shaker with ice and shake until well chilled.
Top with tonic water.
Garnish with orange peel

Mojito
>   3 mint leaves
>   2 oz white rum
>   3/4 oz fresh lime juice
>   1/2 oz simple syrup
>   Club soda to top
>   Mint sprig
>   Lime wheel

Lightly muddle the mint in a shaker.
Add the rum, lime juice, simple syrup and ice and give it a brief shake.
Strain into a highball glass over fresh ice.
Top with the club soda.
Garnish with a mint sprig and lime wheel.

Mai Tai
>   1 1/2 oz spiced rum
>   1 oz coconut rum
>   1/2 oz grenadine
>   3 oz pineapple juice
>   2 oz orange juice

In a cocktail mixer full of ice, combine the spiced rum, coconut rum, grenadine, pineapple juice and orange juice.
Shake vigorously and strain into glass full of ice.

Caribbean Rum Punch
> 1 cup fresh lime juice
> 2 cups simple syrup
> 3 cups spiced rum
> 4 cups orange juice
> 4 dashes Angostura bitters
> Freshly grated nutmeg

In a pitcher, combine lime juice, simple syrup, rum, and orange juice.
Add a few dashes of bitters and some grated nutmeg to taste.
Serve chilled over ice.

Piña Colada
> 2 oz coconut milk
> 2 oz pineapple juice
> 2 oz white rum
> 1/2 oz simple syrup

In a blender, combine coconut milk, pineapple juice, rum, simple syrup, ice.
Blend until smooth.
Pour into glass and serve immediately.

Bahama Mama
> 1 oz white rum
> 1 oz coconut rum
> 1/2 oz grenadine
> 1 oz orange juice
> 1 oz pineapple juice
> Pineapple wedge
> Cherry

Combine all ingredients with crushed ice in an electric blender.
Blend until the drink's consistency is slushy.
Garnish with pineapple wedge and cherry.

Bikini Martini
>1 oz coconut rum
>3/4 oz vodka
>1 oz pineapple juice
>1 splash grenadine
>Orange wheel

Combine rum, vodka, and pineapple juice in a drink shaker.
Shake firmly until frothy.
Pour in a martini glass, add a touch of grenadine in the middle.
Garnish with an orange wheel.

Banana Daquiri
>1/2 banana
>1 1/2 oz white rum
>1 oz lime juice
>1/2 oz triple sec
>1/4 oz simple syrup

Combine banana, light rum, lime juice, triple sec, and sugar in a blender, puree until smooth.
Add ice cubes, and blend on highest setting until slushy, 15 to 20 seconds.
Pour into a glass and serve.

Cherry Bomb
>1 oz white rum
>3 oz lime soda
>1 oz grenadine
>1 oz lime juice
>Lime slice
>Cherry

In a mixing glass combine rum, lime soda, grenadine, and lime juice.
Mix well and pour into a chilled glass.
Garnish with lime slices and cherries.

Whiskey (Bourbon) Cocktails

Old Fashion
>   1/2 teaspoon sugar
>   3 dashes of Angostura bitters
>   Splash of water
>   2 oz bourbon (whiskey)
>   Orange peel

Add the sugar, bitters, and water into a rocks glass, and stir until sugar is nearly dissolved.
Fill the glass with large ice cubes, add the bourbon, and gently stir to combine.
Twist the orange peel over the glass to release the oils, then drop in.

Manhattan
>   2 oz bourbon or rye
>   1 oz sweet vermouth
>   2 dashes Angostura bitters
>   1 dash orange bitter
>   Brandied cherries

Add all the ingredients into a mixing glass with ice and stir until well chilled.
Strain into a chilled martini glass.
Garnish with a brandied cherry.

Gold Rush
>   2 oz bourbon (whiskey)
>   1 oz honey syrup
>   3/4 oz fresh lemon juice
>   Lemon peel

Add all the ingredients into a shaker with ice and shake for 30 seconds.
Strain into a chilled rocks glass with one large ice cube.
Garnish with a lemon peel.

Brown Derby

    1/12 oz bourbon (whiskey)
    1 oz fresh grapefruit juice
    1/2 oz honey syrup
    Grapefruit twist

    Add all ingredients into a shaker with ice and shake.
    Fine strain into a martini glass.
    Express the oil from a grapefruit twist and drop into garnish (or garnish with a grapefruit wedge).

Hot Toddy

    Boiling water, to fill a mug
    4 cloves
    1 lemon peel or wheel
    2 tsp brown sugar
    1/4 oz fresh lemon juice
    2 oz bourbon, rye whiskey, Irish whiskey, or scotch

    Fill a mug with boiling water and let stand for a minute or two to warm.
    Meanwhile, stick the cloves into the lemon peel or wheel and set aside.
    Empty the mug and fill about halfway with fresh boiling water.
    Add the sugar and stir to dissolve.
    Add the prepared lemon peel or wheel and stir.
    Add the lemon juice and whiskey and stir again.

Whiskey Smash

    3 lemon wedges
    2 oz bourbon
    3/4 oz simple syrup
    Mint leaves
    Mint sprig
    Muddle the lemon in a shaker.
    Add the remaining ingredients and ice and shake.
    Double strain into a rocks glass over ice.

Bourbon Rickey
    1 1/2 oz bourbon
    1 lime half
    Sparkling water, to top

    Fill a highball glass with cracked ice.
    Squeeze the lime half into the glass and drop it in.
    Add the bourbon and fill with sparkling water.
    Stir briefly to combine.

Mint Julip
    1/4 oz simple syrup
    8 mint leaves
    2 oz bourbon
    Bitters
    Mint sprig

    In a Julep cup (steel mug) or rocks glass, lightly muddle the mint and syrup.
    Add the bourbon and pack tightly with crushed ice.
    Stir until the cup is frosted on the outside.
    Top with more crushed ice to form an ice dome, and garnish with a mint sprig and a few optional drops of bitters.

Forbidden Sour
    1 oz bourbon
    1 oz grenadine
    1 oz fresh lemon juice
    1/2 oz simple syrup
    Orange wheel
    Cherry

    Add all ingredients into a shaker with ice and shake vigorously.
    Strain into a rocks glass over fresh ice.
    Garnish with an orange wheel and a cherry.

Suffering Bastard

    1 oz bourbon
    1 oz London dry gin
    1/2 oz fresh lime juice
    2 dashes Angostura bitters
    Ginger ale, to top
    Mint sprig

Add the bourbon, gin, lime juice and bitters into a shaker with ice and shake until well chilled (about 30 seconds).
    Strain into a collins glass over fresh ice.
    Top with the ginger ale.

Bourbon Strawberry Iced Tea

    2 large fresh strawberries (sliced into quarters)
    1 oz fresh lemon juice
    2 oz bourbon
    3/4 oz rich simple syrup (2 parts sugar, 1 part water)
    Unsweetened iced tea, to top
    Mint sprig
    Blueberries
    Strawberries

Add the strawberries and lemon juice into a shaker and gently muddle.
    Add the bourbon and simple syrup, add ice, and shake until well chilled.
    Strain into a collins glass over fresh ice.
    Top with unsweetened iced tea.
    Garnish with a mint sprig and skewered blueberries and strawberries.

Tequila Cocktails

Tequila Sunrise
    2 oz blanco tequila
    4 oz fresh orange juice
    1/4 oz grenadine
    Orange slice
    Cherry

Add the tequila and then the orange juice to a chilled highball glass filled with ice.
Top with the grenadine, which will sink to the bottom of the glass, creating a layered effect.
Garnish with an orange slice and a cherry.

Margarita
    2 oz tequila
    1 oz fresh lime juice
    1/2 oz orange liqueur
    1/2 oz agave syrup
    Lime wedge
    Kosher salt

Rub rim of pint glass with lime and salt rim.
Add all the ingredients into a shaker with ice and shake until chilled.
Strain into the prepared rocks glass over fresh ice.
Garnish with a lime wedge.

Samarian Sunset

    1 1/2 oz white rum

    1/2 oz cabbage rum[1]

    3/4 oz triple sec

    3/4 oz simple syrup

    3 oz sparkling water

    3/4 oz grapefruit juice

    1/2 oz lime juice

    1 pinch salt

Chill a large snifter with ice and set aside.

Add the white rum, cabbage rum, triple sec, and simple syrup to a shaker with ice and shake vigorously for 15 seconds.

Strain into the chilled snifter.

Add 3 oz sparkling water.

In a separate container, combine 3/4 oz grapefruit juice and 1/2 oz lime juice.

Pour the juice into the snifter.

Add 1 pinch salt.

Tequila Manhattan

    2 oz reposado tequila

    1 oz sweet vermouth

    2 dashes orange bitters

    Lime twist

Add all the ingredients to a mixing glass and fill with ice.

Stir, and strain into a chilled cocktail glass.

Garnish with a lime twist or a cherry.

---

[1] Cabbage rum: Combine 1/2 head purple cabbage (chopped), with 4 oz white rum in a blender, and blend on high until smooth. Strain using a fine mesh strainer. Makes 4 oz.

Breakfast Margarita
    1 3/4 oz tequila
    3/4 oz fresh lime juice
    3/4 oz Cointreau
    2 tsp orange marmalade
    1/4 oz agave syrup
    1 orange slice

Add all the ingredients to a shaker and fill with ice.
Shake and strain into a rocks glass filled with fresh ice.
Garnish with an orange slice.

Bloody Maria
    2 oz tequila
    4 oz tomato juice
    1/2 oz fresh lemon juice
    4 dashes Worcestershire sauce
    2 dashes Tabasco sauce
    2 dashes Tapatio hot sauce
    1/2 tbsp prepared horseradish, to taste
    1 pinch celery salt
    1 pinch ground black pepper

Garnish:
Lime wedge
Lemon wedge
Cucumber spear
Sweet pepper slices
Jalapeño pepper slices
Queso fresco

Add all the ingredients to a shaker and fill with ice.
Shake briefly and strain into a pint glass filled with fresh ice.
Garnish with a lime wedge, a lemon wedge, a cucumber spear, and a skewer of sweet pepper slices, jalapeño slices and queso fresco.

Paloma

    2 oz tequila
    1/2 oz fresh lime juice
    Grapefruit soda, to top
    Lime wheel

    Add the tequila and lime juice to a highball glass filled with ice.
    Fill with grapefruit soda and stir briefly.

Salty Chihuahua

    2 oz tequila
    4 oz lemonade
    Salt rim
    Lime wedge

    Wet the rim of glass with lime juice, then dip in salt.

    Fill glass with ice.
    Pour in tequila and lemonade.
    Squeeze and drop in the lime wedge.
    Stir.

Screwita (tequila screwdriver)

    2 oz orange juice
    1 oz tequila
    1/2 oz triple sec
    1/2 oz simple syrup
    Splash of lime juice

    Fill a glass with ice.
    Pour the orange juice, tequila, triple sec, sugar, and lime juice over the ice. Stir.

Other Cocktails and Blended Drinks

Mimosa

    2 oz orange juice
    Sparkling wine, chilled

    Pour the orange juice into a champagne flute.
    Fill with sparkling wine.

Long Island Iced Tea

    3/4 oz vodka
    3/4 oz white rum
    3/4 oz silver tequila
    3/4 oz gin
    3/4 oz triple sec
    3/4 oz simple syrup
    3/4 oz fresh lemon juice
    Cola, to top
    Lemon wedge

    Add all ingredients except the cola into a collins glass with ice.
    Top with a splash of the cola and stir briefly.
    Garnish with a lemon wedge.
    Serve with a straw.

Rob Roy

    2 oz scotch
    3/4 oz sweet vermouth
    3 dashes Angostura bitters
    Brandied cherry

    Add all the ingredients into a mixing glass over ice and stir.
    Strain into a chilled cocktail glass.
    Garnish with two speared brandied cherries.

Sidecar

    1 1/2 oz cognac

    3/4 oz orange liqueur (Cointreau or Grand Marnier)

    3/4 oz lemon juice, freshly squeezed

    Orange twist

    Sugar rim (optional)

    Coat the rim of a coupe glass with sugar, if desired, and set aside.

    Add all ingredients into a shaker with ice and shake.

    Strain into the prepared glass.

    Garnish with an orange twist.

Proper Glassware for Cocktails

Highball

A highball glass is a glass tumbler used to serve "tall" cocktails and other mixed drinks that contain a large proportion of a nonalcoholic mixer and are poured over ice. It is often used interchangeably with the collins glass, although the highball glass is shorter and wider in shape.

Examples: *dark "n" stormy, Bloody Mary, mojito, gin and tonic.*

Rocks

The lowball glass, old-fashioned glass, or rocks glass are all names for a short tumbler with a solid base which holds around six to eight ounces of liquid. A solid base aids with drinks that require "muddled" ingredients. These low glasses can also be used for serving a neat pour of liquor.

Examples: *old-fashioned, Negroni, white russian*

Champagne Flute

Sparkling wine needs even less surface area as this will help preserve the bubbles and stop it from going flat too quickly. Hence, the flute glass, with its tall, thin bowl and small mouth. Also used for champagne cocktails.

Examples: *champagne, prosecco, Bellini.*

Hurricane Glass

The Hurricane cocktail, developed by New Orleans tavern owner Pat O'Brien in the 1940s, was first poured into hurricane lamp-shaped glasses, hence the name. The drink and the name stuck, and it has been a mainstay in the French Quarter ever since.

Martini Glass

Martinis were originally served in cocktail glasses (above), but the drink evolved into a variety of vodka-based *tinis* through the '90s, and the serving sizes grew. Martini glasses differ from the traditional cocktail glass by generally having a larger bowl and being fully conical at the bottom.

Margarita Glass

Another specialty drink with its own unique glassware, margaritas were traditionally served in a margarita glass; a "stepped-diameter variant of a cocktail glass." These may be rarely seen in general bars and homes as it has become the norm to serve margaritas in many other vessels, from pint glasses to double old-fashioned glasses.

About the Author

Lou has been bartending on and off since his college days. His first experience came at the Camelot Lounge and Restaurant in the Troy Tower building in New Jersey in 1978. Lou has also worked in the catering division of the Meadowlands Sports Complex, the now MetLife Stadium, as a bartender in the executive-suite level. After moving to Arizona, Lou briefly worked for the Phoenix Suns America West Arena. There, he bartended in the executive suites serving cocktails to the business-sponsored suite customers.

Lou currently bartends at the Northridge Country Club in Fair Oaks, California. Lou has a passion for hosting guests and loves the company of friends and family. Lou was inspired to put this guide together to aid folks sheltering in place during this pandemic. Along with his cookbook *In Lou of Going Out*, Lou hopes to inspire folks to create that *going-out* experience complete with cocktails they would order at their favorite restaurant or bar. Owning his cookbook and cocktail guide will equip you with everything you need to host your own gatherings and create fun memories.

Co-Author

Bar Manager/ Beverage Purchasing Agent; Brad Smith... Has been a food and Beverage professional most of his life, starting out in Reno Nevada working in the casino environment, he moved to Monterey California in 1979 where he worked in various 4 star restaurants, finally ending up at The Pebble Beach Company, where he quickly rose into management, and worked with several famed chef's such as Wolfgang Puck and Emeril Lagasse. Brad moved back to Nor-Cal Fair Oaks area and work for such places as Slocum House, and La Boheme, he joined the NRCC team in 2014 and quickly moved up to Bar Manager, where he has thrived with the goal of providing an unparalleled experience for our members. Brad lives in Fair Oaks with his 17 year old daughter and significant other..

Brad's love of cooking and making craft cocktails drives his passion for throwing small dinner parties for friends and family.